Don't Let The Devil Destroy Your Purpose

by

Roberts Liardon

1st Printing

Don't Let The Devil Destroy Your Purpose
ISBN 1-890900-15-X

Published by Embassy Publishing Co.
P.O. Box 3500
Laguna Hills, California 92654

Contents

1

Discovering Your Purpose

If I sat down with you right now and asked you what your goal is in life, would you be able to tell me? And If you have a goal, is it on it's way to being fulfilled? Everybody needs to discover their purpose in life and fulfill it. There's joy that comes when you find your purpose and begin to pursue it.

I was eight years old when Jesus called me to preach. I was caught up into Heaven for a few hours and I saw the golden street with the golden curbs, and the flowers alongside that hummed because of the surge of new life that kept flowing through them. I was in a praise service and I was in the river of life, I saw some things. At the end of my visitation to Heaven, Christ called me to preach the gospel. He didn't call me just to stay in my hometown,

Tulsa. He said, "I want you to preach while you're yet young. I want you to start preaching while you're a teen-ager."

I said, "Lord, a teenager?"

"That's what I said, a teenager."

Then He said, "I want to promote you, but I can't do it unless you do a few things. If you don't learn to worship Me, and pray in tongues fervently and fight devils, then I can't promote you."

As soon as I came back to earth, there began a war for the purpose of my life.

As soon as you recognize what you're here for, the devil will try to steal it from you. He'll tell you that you're supposed to be a nice, quiet Christian. Or, he'll tell you that you're supposed to pastor a dysfunctional church that is controlled by weirdos!

The devil wants to control you. If he can't control you, then he'll try to kill you. I don't like being controlled, I like to flow.

Some people don't know how to take charge of things. That's why their purpose never comes to pass.

Dealing With Doubting Relatives

When I was growing up, there was a poverty devil that liked our family. It came from grandma and grandpa, down to my mom and dad, and then it tried to get me. In our home, going to McDonalds was like having a steak! We lived like that for many years.

I realized early that the devil doesn't like preachers having money so I'd say, "Devil, let go of my money! It's mine! Poverty devil, you won't destroy me! I know my ministry is going to need *millions* so I'm going to put a stop to you right now! I'll not wait until my ministry gets into a building project or something — I'm going to destroy you right now!"

When I started praying like that, my relatives would say, "Roberts, you pray too much about money!"

"It's because I need a lot of it!" I'd answer, "I refuse to beg from you, so I just beat the devil up, and it comes rolling in nice and easy!"

That was the truth too! Money began coming to me from all over. When I bought myself a new car, some in my family had heart attacks! They began to criticize it; It was too black, it was too gold, it was too nice, it was too sporty.

"Where's your car?" I'd respond.

When they drove up in their used car and I say, "Now which one do you like, yours or this one?"

"Well, I like yours."

"Don't criticize it, then."

Then they got mad and asked, "Why does God give you money?"

"Because I ask Him for it."

"Well, I ask God for money, too."

"Yah, but you don't tell the devil to leave you alone!"

Money Cares Will Destroy Your Purpose

I own that poverty devil that used to own me! I own his territory! When I walk in, he bows! I *never* bow to him! I beat him up! Every time he says, "Don't give," I give double! Every time he tells me *not* to do something, I make sure I do it real bold, in front of him, *on purpose*.

I don't have money cares all over me. That's why I'm able to travel itinerately, preach and have fun. I never look to people as my main source of support. I look to my God and I leave it up to Him to get it to me. I beat up that poverty thinking! I beat up that poverty devil, and he doesn't follow me home anymore!

When the money began rolling in, some of my relatives would say, "Roberts, pray for us and ask God to prosper us."

And I would say, "No! I'm not going to pray for you! You need to go pray for yourself!"

"But, Roberts."

"NO!"

Sometimes relatives think they can control you by putting on a sad face! Watch out for them or they'll get you eventually! Love them, but watch out for them! The devil doesn't use too many strangers, my brother and sister, he uses people you know!

"But, Roberts, you've got faith for money," they'd say.

"You do too!"

"But ours is small."

"That's your fault! You look at yours instead of planting it! You've got yours in a glass case so everybody can come by and look at it! I planted mine and now I've got some trees growing. I'm not going to plant your seed, *plant it yourself!* Fight your own poverty devil! Give to God, worship Jesus, fight devils and learn to enjoy it!"

"But Roberts!"

"Hush!"

You've got to learn to take the upper hand with doubting relatives. Don't let doubting relatives wear you out. They'll kill your faith, if you let them! Just walk away from them, change the subject, or tell them to be quiet.

Sometimes relatives are nosey. You need to push their nose back where it belongs. They like to know everything and they like to read into things. Don't tell them what they don't need to know, it's none of their business.

Nosey relatives will destroy your purpose! Jesus had to deal with nosey relatives. His mother and His brothers came and tried to divert His attention from the call.

Then His mother and brothers came to Him, and could not approach Him because of the crowd. And it was told Him by some, who said, "Your mother and Your brothers are standing outside, desiring to see You." But He answered and said to them, "My mother and My brothers are these who hear the word of God and do it."

Luke 8:19-21 (NKJ)

Jesus' relatives were trying to divert Him from what the Father wanted Him to be doing.

"Well they loved Him," you say.

Yes, but they didn't love Him right! We need to quit having lopsided love! We need to have *straight* love! We need to have *tough* love!

Overcoming Generational Failure

The fear of other relative's failures will destroy your purpose, if you let it. I used to be told that, when I got married, I'd have a divorce in my home. They would say, "Roberts, you're going to do the same stupid thing your father did!"

"I will not!"

"Yes you will!"

"NO!"

I had to fight to keep the divorce spirit off of me! The devil was planning to use the failure of my father to mess up my life and my ministry. He was trying to kill my purpose or destroy the effectiveness of it. Don't ever lose the effectiveness of your purpose! Keep both, your purpose *and* your effectiveness.

Those who know their purpose declare war on the devil and they never give up! They fight! They press on to become a general in God's army. You hold nations inside of you, my brother and sister! Press on and don't give up!

God Is Looking For Nation Changers

God is not just looking for city changers; He's looking for nation changers! We're called to change the world! If you don't learn how to take care of your goofed-up relatives and evil spirits that follow your family, you'll never be able to birth a nation into the kingdom of God. Never! We're not called just to change Moscow, London and Los Angeles, we're called to change the world! You've got to keep fighting the things that try to kill your purpose, and you must never give up!

I don't just travel around the world and have nice little meetings, I preach loud and bold because I have nations inside of me! When I stand before God, I'll have reached whole nations for Him! It is because I've wrestled with certain devils and won!

I'm not on the earth to be a nice preacher, I'm here to be an invader! And I'm not going to give up until I win! I'm not going to fade away, I'm going to go out with a blast! I'm going to start with one too!

There comes a day when you have to decide to follow your purpose. There comes a day when you've got to say, "Alright, this is my purpose and it starts now!" Your purpose starts when you give your full attention to it, not half your attention!

Many today are comfortable. They are sitting around waiting to hear from Heaven. But Mark already heard from Heaven for us. He said *"Go!"* (Mark 16:15)

People that sit around waiting for things to happen will never preach the gospel to the nations. They will never truly enjoy their life, or give big gifts to churches to help humanity. They need a purpose and a vision from God.

Big Words and No Action

The devil wants you to be nothing but a big mouth with no feet! Those who discover their purpose and call, and begin to go for it, will be fought by devils and humans. When I told my family that God wanted me to preach while I was still young, they said, "Are you serious?"

When I said, "Yes!" they began to have discussions behind my back. They'd say, "He can't do that! Grandma makes him preach, Grandma put that in him."

No, *God* put it in me, Grandma only helped develop it.

They kept saying, "Roberts, be normal! You don't have to preach, go be a basketball player and date dizzy blondes!"

And I used to answer by saying, "I know I'm a little bit strange, but I'm not changing!" Then God corrected me one day. He said, "Roberts, quit agreeing with a lie! Every time that someone says you're different, and you agree with them, you're agreeing with a lie. Anybody that obeys My will, in the present time, is not weird, they're normal. Those who don't are the weirdos!"

So I changed the way I answered people.

When they would say, "Roberts, your weird."

I'd say, "No, I'm normal, *you're* the weirdo!"

2

Pursuing Your Purpose

Some people think that being a minister is not the greatest occupation, but it's higher than the presidency!

Some of you look at the ministry as an occupation that is easy. No! Do you think that being a preacher is easy? You're crazy! Do you think pastoring a church is wonderful? It's *work* my friends! It takes *effort* to cause your purpose to happen.

When I was a teenager the Lord said, "I want you to start preaching, *now.*"

"Lord, I don't even know how to write a sermon."

"That's okay, I'll give you one and I'll open up doors for you."

That's how my ministry operates. I have never begged for one meeting in my life, and I've never begged for one dime. I don't believe the righteous are to beg. It's alright to present what you're doing so the people can have the opportunity to give. That's fine. But if you're truly obeying God, you won't have to beg.

Purpose takes you out of the arena of the soul and puts you in the arena of faith and adventure. A lot of people have no adventure in their life because they have no purpose.

Regaining Your Sense of Adventure

There was a time in my life when I was losing my sense of adventure. I thought, "Lord, I'm tired of all these airplanes and hotel rooms."

(After the 6,000th hotel room, they all look the same. After spending thousands of hours in the air with rude stewardesses, believe me, it gets old.)

"God, I've got to have joy — I'm too young to be bored! I've preached to the twenty person crowd and I've preached to the crowds of thousands. I've been shot at, I've seen people dying, I've seen food that still moves, and I ate it and I didn't gripe! I've been in hundreds of cities and I've spoken with presidents and I'm only 21 — Lord we've got to have some more fun here! I'm too young to have the world of ministry be boring to me!"

"Roberts," God said, "What have I called you to do?"

I told Him what I knew. Then He said, "Don't you think I've got more for you than that? Don't you think that I know what you're like? I'd blow you away if I told you everything I want for you to do. I only give you a little at a time. The faster you do some things, the more you'll get to do in your life."

There are some things that are set in the timings of God, but there are some things you can accomplish at your own pace.

You see, people like to be you're best friend you when you're successful. They don't care when you're a nobody. But when you start experiencing some success, everybody wants to help you. You know why? Because they don't know how to help themselves. They don't know what their life is for. They don't know their purpose.

No one cared who Roberts Liardon was, until I wrote my first book, and it made number one in sales. No one cared who Roberts Liardon was, until cripples started walking and God started showing up. Then they started saying, "Who is this guy — where did he come from?" They'd come and sit in the back row of my meetings and stare. They didn't want to invite me to preach in their church, until they felt I was okay.

Once, I had a man approach me and say, "I'm cautiously excited about you."

When you know God and you know your purpose in life, you're boldness will make people nervous. You will do things faster and more successfully than most.

I knew what I was called to do from the day I returned from Heaven. I didn't have to wait twenty years to find out. I knew that I was called to preach. I didn't want to be a businessman, I didn't want to be an airplane pilot, I wanted to be a preacher, and I wanted to preach boldly and passionately! I like that, that's my call, that's my purpose in the earth, and nobody can take it away from me! I don't care how many lies people tell about me, I don't care what they all gossip about — I can't be stopped! I know my call. I know my duty. When you know you're obeying God, nothing can stop you!

Religious Confrontations

I had a minister try to stop me one time. He didn't like me because I disturbed his world. I was a little bit too bold for him. He's one of these soulish preachers. He'd love everybody with a false kind of love. He would never tell a homosexual to get free. He would never tell an intellectual to get out of their head and get in their heart. He would just love them with a soulish type of love that does nothing for nobody. When I came along and began confronting people's problems he'd say, "Roberts, you've got to walk in love."

"I am."

"Well, love does not confront."

"God does."

"Well, love never causes people to get mad."

"God does. His love caused Him to tell the Pharisees that their father was the devil! (John 8:44) That's always good news! He also went in the temple one time and kicked out all the money changers, and said, 'Get out!' Now that's *tough love.*"

Somehow we forget those kinds of things.

Paul had great love. He wrote in his writings, *"You call me your enemy because I write and tell you the truth!"* (Gal 4:16) Some of you say, *"I'm just wild with my pen, but I'm not wild in person. Wait until I get there."* (2 Cor 10:10-11) *"I confronted Peter to his face, because he was to blame!"* (Gal 2:11)

You see, those who know their God and their purpose, do not live in wonder-wonder land. If you're always saying, "I wonder what's going to happen, I wonder when these things are going to occur," they will never happen! Purpose means you make it happen! With your faith, with your feet and with the power that God has invested in you.

3

Protecting Your Purpose

What destroys purpose? Evil people! Evil people will destroy the purpose of God in your life! What is the definition of an evil person? Anybody that works against the will of God!

"Roberts, you have to love people."

I love them, but I'm not going to let them destroy what God is building! We've got to be like Paul who said, *"...I am set for the defense of the gospel."* Phil 1:17 (KJV) We are supposed to be watchman who stop the attacks of the devil.

I've had a lot of encounters with 'false brethren' who wanted to be my friend and help me. They came and said, "Roberts we see that you have a *great* ministry, and we can see that God's hand is *greatly* upon you." (They always say that!)

The devil *hates* an individual that knows their purpose and their call! He will send evil people to flatter you! They will say things like, "You're one of the greatest preachers I've ever heard in my life!" And you both know that that's not the truth!

Then, if the devil can't get you through a human being, he'll try to get you himself. This is where lots of ministries die. Satan bombards them in the realm of the spirit and wears them out. When God puts a vision inside your heart the devil will say, "You can't do that!" You need to rise up and say, "Devil, you're a liar, go away from me! God is able to perform what He has said! I'll do it, and I'll do it on time, I'll do it right and I'll do it first class!"

The devil always wants you to go coach. But if you obey God boldly, He'll give you a first class ticket! But you've got to prove out to Him.

Don't Share Your Vision With Just Anybody

The third thing that hinders the purpose of God in your life is; *others knowing it.* Joseph was a good example of this. He told his brothers what was going to happen and they came out against him, to destroy him. (Gen 37:20) When you share your vision with certain people, they'll destroy it, if you let them. You've got to learn how to deal with human beings. Some are nice, some are mean, some are dumb, some are sly, and some are real. You have to learn how to deal with them, because we live in a world of human beings. When you start doing what God has called you to do, some will jump on your bandwagon and others will try to stop you.

Why do human beings get mad at people that know what they're doing? Why do they criticize them and lie about them? It's because it makes them feel guilty for not knowing themselves what they're called to do! Some have gotten to the place where they believe the way they live is the way God wants them to live. When you step out and do something that disturbs their world, they'll either have to say it's of the devil, or admit that they're wrong.

Misunderstandings

Another thing that destroys purpose, is misunderstandings. Being misunderstood can hurt your heart and cause you to let go of a vision. One of the greatest problems in ministry today is the area of misunderstanding. Settle it right now, when you preach the gospel, you are going to be misunderstood. People are going to believe that you said things you didn't say and then get twenty other people believing it, too. They'll come out ready to stone you. If you don't watch it, their misunderstanding will destroy the joy of your purpose. Always remember that joy is a protection of your purpose. You've got to watch out for misunderstandings. Just learn that people sometimes like to misunderstand things, for their own benefit.

Laziness Will Destroy Purpose

Another thing that destroys purpose is laziness. Laziness is when you do nothing, but think you did a lot.

Have you ever noticed that a lazy person will never say he's lazy. They'll say, "Oh, I've been working, I've been doing things!" But when you ask to see the products of his work, he doesn't have any. I know a lot of people like that. They say, "I've been really out there working for God."

"Well, How many people did you talk to?" I'll ask.

"Oh, Well, ahhhh, how's the weather? I had intercession on me today."

"How long did you pray?"

"Oh."

"Oh? Oh what? Give me a figure."

"Well, I, I, I had to do something around the house."

Well, what did you do?"

"Well."

That's the way a lot of people live, and they call that purpose. That's nothing but laziness. Laziness will destroy your purpose in life! Laziness will cause you to be mentally wore out, but never accomplish anything. Laziness will cause you to think a lot, and talk a lot, but never do anything worthwhile for God.

Restlessness

Another thing that destroys a purpose is a restless spirit. A restless spirit will cause you to do things before the right timing of God.

Many of the people that I've helped train want to be great ministers tomorrow afternoon, but they don't know one thing about praying for a sick person. They don't know how to pray for an epileptic. They don't know how to pray for the insane person. They have not been instructed.

Others want to go out and be Billy Graham and win thousands of souls, but they're scared to talk to their next door neighbor. There's something wrong with this picture. You need to start where you're at and grow from there.

My ministry started in my bedroom, with one small desk and an empty calendar that I talked to everyday. I'd look at my desk and say, "Grow!" I'd look at the world map on my wall and say, "Open!" I'd look at my calendar and said, "One day you'll be too small, you won't be large enough! There won't be enough days in you for me to go where I have to go, and what I have to do!"

Despair and Frustration

Another thing that destroys purpose, is despair and frustration. The devil *loves* to try and get you frustrated. If he can get you frustrated and mentally tormented, he'll kill your purpose for living. He'll rob it from your heart, your eyes and from your feet. You've got to watch your frustration and stress level. Always stay happy and act like you know what you're doing — *that's called faith!*

When I first started preaching, I didn't know how to preach or pray for sick people, I only had faith. I knew my faith and the Holy Spirit would cause everything to turn out right.

Many times, the devil would try to bombard me before my meetings. He'd say, "What are you going to preach on? What are you going to do?"

I don't like when people ask me what I'm going to preach on, because half the time, I don't know. That shocks some people, but that's just the way I operate. I write lots of little notes, but I hardly ever use them. I study to show myself approved and then I come out and let it roll. (2 Tim 2:15) If it flows a different way, then my notes don't go with me. I like to speak by inspiration.

So, before my meetings, the devil will try to frustrate me. He'll say, "What are you going to preach on? You've got a thousand people out there and this is the first time you're in this church — you better know what you're going to preach on, or you might not be invited back." The devil will say those kinds of things to frustrate me. He'll say, "Well, who said you could write this book and that people will want it? Who said you could start preaching when you're young?"

Listening to those kinds of things will rob you of your purpose. I stopped them by saying, "Devil, you're a liar! I'm called to preach, when I step onto the platform, I'll preach and you'll leave! I'll have a good time and I'll be invited back too! You're a liar! Get away from me! Go and get yourself a front row seat so you can hear me preach!"

4

Perfecting Your Purpose

Don't ever doubt your purpose! Don't ever doubt your call! Continue growing into it! Don't look around! Carry it and hold tightly to it!

Many never fulfill their destiny because they don't know how to carry it and they don't know how to present it. Their destiny weighs them down and they get weak and worn out.

Destiny always means war, my brother and sister! Destiny is a boat going against the current. It's not always easy, but if you know the Lord, you can have fun pursuing it. Don't let the devil wear you out. If the devil can wear you out, he'll own you. Don't ever get worn out! Stay strong in joy, strong in faith and strong in boldness!

Boldness is an atomic bomb in the spirit! That's why I preach loud, bold and direct. I don't preach to make people like me, I preach to help people change.

I don't live in a world of wondering, I live in a world of knowing! I know where I am, I know who I am, and I know where I'm going! That's why, ten years from now, I'll have something, while others will still be standing around and hoping for it.

Make A Decision!

When I go to colleges and speak, it bothers me that many of the students don't know what they're going to be. They go from science majors to math majors, from this to that. They spend half their life in school, paying thousands of dollars and never knowing what they're going to be. Somehow I wonder if they'll ever get there. They're professional students. They don't have the faith, guts, or strength to say, "This is what I am and this is where I'm going!"

When I was a teenager, I told my family that I was a preacher. They said, "Well, what about school?"

"What about it?" I retorted, "I'll finish high school, but I'm in two schools right now. I'm in a school of Holy Ghost and knees and a school of mental academics."

"Well you're going to have a little bit more."

"I'm going to get it from Heaven!"

"What do you mean, from Heaven?"

"Just what I said! I'm going to get it from Heaven! Some people need to go to college, and God calls them. But God told me He wants to put me in the ministry NOW!"

I've never spent one day of my life out of reach of my destiny. Even when I'm on vacation, my destiny is still thriving inside of me. I never let go of it — it's my life! If I let go of my destiny, I become a plain empty shell. I keep it inside of me, I live with a purpose — I have a meaning.

I've always been a direct person — a very bold person — and I have never cared what people thought. If someone doesn't like me, whoopy-do! If someone does, whoopy-do! I don't worry about all that because I learned a secret about people; *they're fickle*. One day you're great, and the next day you're a dog! One day they're ready to give you a thousand dollars to help you go to Africa, and the next day they want to take it back! I love people, but I never let them bug me!

Take The Narrow Road

Those who live in destiny will lose many friends in their life. If you don't have guts to say "good-bye," to some of your friends, you'll never see your destiny fulfilled. You'll have to say good-bye to many friends, in your lifetime.

The Bible says that there is a broad road that leads to destruction — it's the narrow one that leads to Heaven! (Mat 7:13) Your destiny is on that narrow road! Anybody can walk with all their goofed-up friends down the broad road, but only one person can walk up that narrow road; *you.*

Destiny causes crossroads. I've faced many crossroads in my life. What is a crossroad? It's a time when you've got to make a decision which way you're going to go, and evaluate each result.

Standing At The Crossroads

I grew up with five friends in a Pentecostal holiness church, and I liked them a whole lot. They were my buddies. But when the call of God came to me, it scared my pastor and youth pastor because it immediately came with power. When the Spirit of God would come on me, it would knock everybody out. At 13 years of age, I scared 1,200 Pentecostal holiness adults. I was called on the pastoral carpet and told not to touch anybody. I quit touching them and they all fell over anyway! They didn't know what to do with me. They kept criticizing me and coming against me. I came to a crossroad — my whole family did. I had to decide whether or not to stay with my five friends in that church, or follow the call of God and live.

Some people said, "You should stay here and learn." But they really didn't want me to stay; they wanted me to die! They wanted me to develop a big head and not a big heart. They wanted me to be nice and not bold. That's what they wanted. So I said, "Goodbye!" I went to Victory Christian Center across town. They helped me a lot. That's one reason why I'm here today. They saw my call, believed in it and helped me develop it.

Don't Become a Hollywood Production

To live in purpose is to live a life that's real. What you see is what you get. When I walk down off the stage, I'm the same Roberts. When I'm on Piedmont, I'm the same Roberts. I don't change. There may be a little difference because of the anointing, but not much. I try to live the way I preach, and I try to preach the way I live. If I didn't, I'd be a two-faced liar!

Don't ever let your life be a Hollywood production. Live your life the way you are with God, and grow. If you're anything like me, you don't like people who aren't real. That's why you don't go to certain churches and you don't like certain ministries — *they bug you*. They bug me too! Their ministry is a Hollywood production instead of a life that's real. And they never produce miracles for people. But you will!

BOOKS
by Roberts Liardon

A Call To Action

Cry Of The Spirit

Extremists, Radicals and Non-Conformists

Final Approach

Forget Not His Benefits

God's Generals

Haunted Houses, Ghosts, And Demons

Holding To The Word of The Lord

I Saw Heaven

Kathryn Kuhlman

Knowing People By The Spirit

On Her Knees

Religious Politics

Run To The Battle

School of The Spirit

Sharpening Your Discernment

Smith Wigglesworth - Complete Collection

Smith Wigglesworth Speaks To Students

Spiritual Timing

The Invading Force

The Most Dangerous Place To Be

The Price of Spiritual Power

The Quest For Spiritual Hunger

Three Outs and You're In

*To place an order call (949) 833-3555
or visit our website at: www.robertsliardon.org*

Spirit Life Partner

Roberts Liardon

Wouldn't It Be Great...

- If you could send 500 missionaries to the nations of the earth?
- If you could travel 250,000 air miles, boldly preaching the Word of God in 93 nations?
- If you could strengthen and train the next generation of God's leaders?
- If you could translate 23 books and distribute them into 37 countries?

...Now You Can!

Maybe you can't go, but by supporting this ministry every month, your gift can help to communicate the gospel around the world.

Roberts Liardon Ministries is sending Gospel missionaries to the hard and remote places of the earth!

---- CLIP ALONG LINE & MAIL TO ROBERTS LIARDON MINISTRIES. ----

☐ **YES!!** Pastor Roberts, I want to support your work in the kingdom of God by becoming a **SPIRIT LIFE PARTNER.** Please find enclosed my first monthly gift.

Name _____

Address _____

City _____ State _____ Zip _____

Phone (_____) _____

SPIRIT LIFE PARTNER AMOUNT: $ _____

☐ Check / Money Order   ☐ VISA   ☐ American Express   ☐ Discover   ☐ MasterCard

☐☐☐☐☐ ☐☐☐☐ ☐☐☐☐ ☐☐☐☐

Name On Card_____ Exp. Date____/____/____

Signature_____ Date ____/____/____

Roberts Liardon Ministries

P.O. Box 30710 ♦ Laguna Hills, CA 92654 ♦ (949) 833-3555 ♦ Fax (949) 833.9555 ♦ www.robertsliardon.org

AUDIO TAPES *by Roberts Liardon*

Acts of The Holy Spirit

Be Strong In The Lord

Breaking the Cycle of Failure

Changing Spiritual Climates

God's Secret Agents

Haunted Houses, Ghosts, & Demons

How To Combat Demonic Forces

How To Stay On The Mountaintop

How To Stir Up Your Calling
and Walk In Your Gifts

How To Survive An Attack

Increasing Your Spiritual Capacity

I Saw Heaven

Life & Ministry of Kathryn Kuhlman

Living On The Offensive

No More Religion

Obtaining Your Financial Harvest

Occupy 'Til He Comes

Personality of the Holy Spirit

Prayer 1 - How I Learned To Pray

Prayer 2 - Lost In The Spirit

Reformers & Revivalists

Rivers of Living Water (Grams)

School of The Spirit

Seven Steps of Demonic Posession

Sharpening Your Discernment (One)

Sharpening Your Discernment (Two)

Spirit Life

Spiritual Climates

Storms of His Presence

Taking A City

Tired? How To Live In The
Divine Life of God

True Spiritual Strength

The Anointing

The Healing Evangelists

The Charges of St. Paul - 1 Timothy

The Charges of St. Paul - 2 Timothy

The Working of Miracles
& Divine Health

Three Arenas of Authority
& Conflict

Three Worlds: God, You,
& The Devil

Tired? How To Live In The
Divine Life Of God

Tongues And Their Diversities

True Spiritual Strength

Useable Faith

Victorious Living In The Last Days

Working The Word

What You Need To Keep
Under To Go Over

Your Faith Stops The Devil

*To place an order call (949) 833-3555
or visit our website at: www.robertsliardon.org*

Seven reasons you should attend Spirit Life Bible College

1. SLBC is a **spiritual school** with an academic support; not an academic school with a spiritual touch.

2. SLBC teachers are **successful ministers** in their own right. Pastor Roberts Liardon will not allow failure to be imparted into his students.

3. SLBC is a member of **Oral Roberts University Educational Fellowship** and is **fully accredited** by the International Christian Accreditation Association.

4. SLBC hosts monthly seminars with some of the **world's greatest** ministers who add another element, anointing and impartation to the students' lives.

5. Roberts Liardon understands your commitment to come to SLBC and commits himself to students by **ministering weekly** in classroom settings.

6. SLBC provides **hands-on** ministerial training.

7. SLBC provides ministry opportunity through its **post-graduate placement program**.

Send for your **FREE Video** of Spirit Life Bible College today!

-------------------- CLIP ALONG LINE & MAIL TO ROBERTS LIARDON MINISTRIES. --------------------

☐ **YES!** Pastor Roberts, please rush me a **FREE VIDEO** and information packet for **SPIRIT LIFE BIBLE COLLEGE**.

Name _____

Address _____

City _____ State _____ Zip _____

Phone (_____) _____

Roberts Liardon Ministries
P.O. Box 30710 ◆ Laguna Hills, CA 92654-0710
(949) 833.3555 ◆ Fax (949) 833.9555
www.robertsliardon.org

VIDEO TAPES *by Roberts Liardon*

2+2=4

And The Cloud Came

A New Generation

Apostles, Prophets
    & Territorial Churches

Apostolic Alignment

Are You A Prophet?

Confronting The Brazen Heavens

Developing An Excellent Spirit

Don't Break Rank

Does Your Pastor Carry A Knife?

Forget Not His Benefits

God's Explosive Weapons

How To Be An End Time Servant

How To Be Healed
    of Spiritual Blindness

I Saw Heaven

Ministering To The Lord

No More Walls

Reformers And Revivalists (5 Vol.)

Spirit of Evangelism

The Importance of Praying
    In Tongues

The Lord Is A Warrior

The Most Dangerous Place To Be

The New Millennium Roar

The Operation of Exhortation

The Word of The Lord Came
    Unto Me Saying

True And False Manifestations

Was Jesus Religious?

Why God Wrote Verse 28

New God's Generals Video Collection

Volume 1 - John Alexander Dowie

Volume 2 - Maria Woodworth-Etter

Volume 3 - Evan Roberts

Volume 4 - Charles F. Parham &
    William J. Seymour

Volume 5 - John G. Lake

Volume 6 - Smith Wigglesworth

Volume 7 - Aimee Semple
    McPherson

Volume 8 - William Branham

Volume 9 - Jack Coe

Volume 10 - A. A. Allen

Volume 11 - Kathryn Kuhlman

Volume 12 - Highlights
    & Live Footage

Videos by Gladoylene Moore (Grams)

Foundations of Stone

God of the Breakthrough

How I Learned To Pray

How To Avoid Disaster

Seeking God

The Prophetic Flow

The Sword Of Gideon

The Warrior Names of God

*To place an order call (949) 833-3555
or visit our website at: www.robertsliardon.org*

ROBERTS LIARDON MINISTRIES
INTERNATIONAL OFFICES

EUROPE
Roberts Liardon Ministries
P.O. Box 295
Welwyn Garden City
AL7 2ZG
England
011-44-1707-327-222

SOUTH AFRICA
Roberts Liardon Ministries
P.O. Box 3155
Kimberely 8300
South Africa
011-27-53-832-1207

AUSTRALIA
Roberts Liardon Ministries
P.O. Box 7
Kingsgrove, NSW
1480
Australia
011-61-500-555-056

Roberts Liardon Ministries

P.O. Box 30710
Laguna Hills, California, USA
92654-0710
Telephone: (949) 833-3555
Fax: (949) 833-9555
Visit our website at: www.robertsliardon.org